THE HEART OF GOLD

THE HEART OF GOLD

HEMALATHA GNANASEKAR

GenNext Publication

First Published, 2018

Published by
GenNext Publication
5, Ansari Road
Daryaganj, New Delhi-110002
Phone: 9811692060
E-mail: gennextpublication@hotmail.com

Printed at: G. Print Process, Delhi.

Cataloging in Publication Data—DK
Courtesy: D.K. Agencies (P) Ltd. <docinfo@dkagencies.com>

Gnanasekar, Hemalatha, 1965- **author.**
The heart of gold / Hemalatha Gnanasekar.
pages cm
Novel.
ISBN 9789380223407

1. Indic fiction (English) I. Title.

LCC PR9499.4.G53H43 2018 | DDC 823.92 23

DEDICATED TO

SHIRDI SAI BABA

CONTENTS

PRELUDE

Mukesh is rudely awakened from his dream about a life of marital bliss when Nithya, his newly-wed wife, tells him that her parents had resorted to emotional blackmail and forced her into this marriage. Instead of the love and companionship for which he had hoped, he finds only anger and resentment. To make matters worse, on a clandestine rendezvous with her boyfriend, Nithya lands herself in serious trouble.

Will Mukesh help extricate her from the dangerous situation she finds herself? Can they put the past behind them and find love and togetherness in each other?

The Heart of Gold reflects the changing times as Indian cities transform into multicultural metropolises and young people try to navigate the confusing landscape, with traditional values on one side and the rising aspirations of a fast-paced global lifestyle on the other.

CHAPTER ONE

Mukesh was having a bath when he heard his cell phone buzz. He ignored it. He cursed his mother for having talked him into marrying a girl ten years younger than him, despite his protests that their viewpoints would be incompatible. Although he had borne all his young wife's tantrums and wayward behavior patiently, she had left him. Mukesh was heart-broken now. His marriage had lasted only six months. All his efforts to salvage it had been futile.

He had switched off his cell phone the previous afternoon. Ever since he had read Nithya's dreadfully final note, his mind had been in turmoil and he wanted to shut the world out. If only he had not been quite so accommodating and adjustable with his young wife's vagaries, things would never have come to such a pass. But the damage was irrevocable and all he could do now was to reconcile himself to the broken relationship and move on.

It was only early that morning that he had switched his mobile back on and he was already regretting it. He stood under the shower for a long time, letting the cold-water flow over his body, but it did little to soothe his turbulent thoughts.

When he stepped into the bedroom, toweling his rather slim body, the phone was still ringing. Irritated, he picked it up, then froze when he noticed the caller ID.

Nithya. What did she want from him now? Hadn't she caused enough agony already! He disconnected the call; almost immediately, the phone rang again. He let it ring for a minute or so before finally giving in. 'What do you want?' he asked gruffly.

In response, all he could hear were sobs. Frustrated, he yelled, 'Who is this?'

Between sobs, Nithya said, 'Mukesh ... please ... please ... don't hang up.'

He snorted angrily.

'Mukesh ... listen to me, please. I'm in trouble. I need your help.'

'Is that so?' he asked sarcastically.

Nithya sniffed and cleared her throat. 'Mukesh ... please note down this address and come quickly.'

'Nithya,' Mukesh said, 'you and I are finished, remember? So this, whatever it is, is none of my business!'

'Mukesh, please,' she cried, beseechingly, 'I don't know how much time I have.' She dropped her voice to a whisper. 'I cannot talk now. I'll explain everything in detail later. Now, please, please, write this address down, and come here as soon as you can.'

As Mukesh desultorily scribbled the address on a bit of paper, the phone went dead.

Mukesh stared at the address blankly for a while before crumpling the piece of paper and flinging it into the bin. If Nithya was in trouble, she deserved it.

CHAPTER TWO

'What the hell is wrong with you, Ma! Have you lost your mind?' said Mukesh peevishly.

This was nothing new to Lakshmi. Whenever she broached the subject of his marriage, Mukesh would lose his temper. Under one pretext or another, he had been refusing to get married. However, one day, when he noticed his mother looking extremely morose and depressed, he sat her down and explained the reason for his reluctance to commit to matrimony.

'Ma, please don't keep pestering me to get married. I'd like to make sure that my career is stabilized first – as a matter of fact, I'm due for a promotion shortly. As soon as I get the management post, I'll be happy to settle down with a wife. Until such time, please don't mention this topic again.' Three months after this assurance to his mother, Mukesh got his promotion. He was now the Manager and heading the software development and maintenance division of a Multinational I.T company. Now, Lakshmi was not prepared to wait any longer.

Moreover, Priya, Mukesh's older sister, lived in Coimbatore with her husband and their two, lusty sons – both under the age of five. She telephoned her mother often to give her updates about her young family. With her family's increasing needs, she had decided to supplement her husband's income by taking up a job herself. She wanted her mother to move in with her family in Coimbatore to babysit her children while she was away at work. However, Lakshmi wanted to see her son settled down with a wife before moving out to live with her daughter.

One early morning, Lakshmi was cutting vegetables to prepare fried rice for Mukesh when her cell phone rang. It was from her daughter.

On hearing about her brother's promotion, Priya immediately called her mother and once again requested her to come and settle down with her. When her mother gave her the same reply that she would come and stay with her once she was able to finalize Mukesh's marriage, she was rather cut up.

She yelled at her mother, "Ma, now is the right time. Don't listen to any excuses Mukesh gives you. Just go ahead and fix up his marriage."

"Well Priya... I am also seriously thinking about that..."

Not letting her finish, Priya continued heatedly, "Ma, now that Mukesh has got his promotion, what is holding him from getting married ? Is he afraid of a committed life ? Just don't get cowed down by his threats and go ahead and fix up his marriage. Things will slowly fall in line."

"Priya...you are right ! I will start looking for a suitable girl for him and hope God doesn't let me down!"

Lakshmi was now bent upon finding a suitable girl for her son. She, at once, registered Mukesh's name in a Match Making center in West Mambalam, even without informing him.

The first caller was a middle-aged lady who introduced herself as Parvathi. She informed Lakshmi that she was staying in Kodambakkam and expressed interest in this alliance. She spoke to her kindly thus leaving an indelible impression in Lakshmi's mind. Both women decided to meet in person and discuss further on the next day itself.

Mukesh was unaware that his mother had gone ahead and registered his name in a matrimonial matchmaking center. Lakshmi wished to keep the whole thing a secret until she was able to finalize everything. So, the next day, after Mukesh left for work, Lakshmi went to see Parvathi. Parvathi was a stylish woman with a kind face. She greeted Lakshmi with a warm smile and the two ladies spent almost half a day talking and sharing details about their lives. Lakshmi was quite taken with Nithya, Parvathi's daughter. Nithya, twenty-one years old, light-skinned and beautiful, was exactly the girl for Mukesh. After promising them that she would visit again with her son during the weekend, Lakshmi left the house brimming with happiness.

That evening, Lakshmi was bubbling with excitement and could hardly wait to tell Mukesh all about her day. He had barely stepped into the house after a busy day in the office, when his mother began fussing and cooing over him. She plied him with homemade pastries, sweetmeats and a steaming cup of coffee.

'So, what's the special occasion today?' he asked, grinning.

Lakshmi told him all about Parvathi, and more importantly, the beautiful Nithya.

Mukesh, however, reacted with his typical impatience. This time, however, Lakshmi refused to back down. She only paused to wonder whether Priya was possibly right about Mukesh having a commitment phobia. Determined not to falter in her mission to get her son to tie the knot she brushed aside her son's choler. It was imperative that she go to Coimbatore to help in her daughter's household and Lakshmi was set on doing so with an easy mind.

'Mukesh, I refuse to listen to your excuses any more. Tell me one plausible reason for refusing this proposal and I shall never again talk to you about marriage.'

'Ma, don't be so naïve. Aren't you aware of the reason?' Mukesh reproached her.

Lakshmi blinked uncomprehendingly.

'This girl is ten years younger than me, Ma. It's more than likely that we have very different tastes and outlooks given the gap in our ages. How could we possibly be happy together?'

Lakshmi heaved a sigh of relief. At least, Mukesh was not dismissing the match out of hand. This time he was merely quibbling about the Nithya's extreme youth.

'The age gap is actually a blessing in disguise, don't you see? An older woman might tend to be domineering and overbearing creating frequent ego clashes between the two of you ... and you being so short-tempered ...'

Mukesh was annoyed at her silly justification. He changed tack as he interrupted her, 'Don't you know that it has been my long-cherished dream to be an ideal husband – to marry someone from a very poor family, with no dowry?'

Lakshmi had a pat answer for this and butted in, 'Oh, we won't take any dowry. I told the girl's mother that. The poor woman was distraught that all the jewellery she had kept aside for her daughter's wedding was recently stolen when a burglar broke into their apartment.

I consoled her saying that we'd like a simple wedding as well ... She was most grateful.'

I'm sure she was, thought Mukesh cynically. Although he did not contradict her, he was still irritated by his mother's high-handedness. 'You seem to have finalized everything without bothering to consult me.'

But Lakshmi was unfazed and said excitedly, 'Listen, Mukesh, this girl is so beautiful, when you see her, you will fall head over heels in love with her.'

'Ma, stop building castles in the air! Whether I fall head over heels in love or fall flat on my face, is for me to decide,' he said, thoroughly annoyed by now.

'Mukesh, please, there is no turning back now. I have already conveyed our acceptance, so please, please, do not let me down.'

Lakshmi made a dramatic exit at this point and rushed out of the room with tears streaming down her face. Mukesh sat looking at her nonplussed before reaching for another pastry.

CHAPTER THREE

Nithya lay sprawled on the bed fast asleep. Mukesh, admiring her curvy figure, stood beside the bed wondering whether he should wake her up.

It was their wedding night and he had been at the point of entering the honeymoon suite when his phone rang. It was his boss, who had launched into a long-drawn explanation and apologized profusely for not having been able to make it to the wedding.

Ten interminably long minutes later, when Mukesh entered the room, he found that his bride was already slumbering soundly.

He dragged a chair over, hoping the clatter would wake her up. It didn't. He glanced around as he sat down and was surprised to see a plate with a half-eaten apple and a bunch of grapes on the nightstand. A glass tumbler, half full of milk, stood beside the plate. Some grape seeds on the floor crunched underfoot. They bore mute testimony to the young bride's very late dinner. She must have been famished after the long wedding ceremony, thought Mukesh. Or was she merely staving off her boredom by nibbling on whatever was available? Whatever the case was, she had cared enough to have left something for him.

Mukesh took a bite of the remaining half of the apple. He finished what was left of the grapes as well and downed the milk in the glass. He replaced the plate and tumbler on the bedside table with a thud. His sleeping bride did not stir.

He sat there for a while wishing that by some miracle Nithya would wake up. After a little while, feeling rather drowsy himself, he stood up, stretched and yawned. One of her slim legs was dangling over the side of the bed. He tenderly lifted and placed it on the bed. He switched off the light and lay down silently beside her.

His first night had been an utter fiasco because of his long-winded boss. He consoled himself with the thought that there would always be a second chance tomorrow. Nithya was his wife after all and they had their whole lives ahead of them.

CHAPTER FOUR

It was 5.30 in the morning when Nithya woke up the following day. Mukesh was snoring softly when she quietly left the room, bathed and freshened up. After about an hour, she returned with Mukesh's coffee and hesitantly nudged his shoulder to wake him up. Mukesh sat up rubbing his eyes, feeling vaguely startled. He smiled as he became fully awake and recognized the vision that stood by the bed with the steaming beverage.

Mukesh took the cup of coffee from her and placed it on the nightstand. He reached for her hand and patted the bed by his side. Nithya turned away from him shyly but Mukesh gently drew her down to sit beside him.

When she was seated, he sipped his coffee and asked, 'Did you sleep well last night?'

'No,' she said.

He was taken aback by her bluntness. He sipped his coffee in the uncomfortable silence, and then asked, 'Why?'

'I had a bad dream.' More silence.

Taking the cup from him, Nithya stood up to leave. However, Mukesh gently pulled her back to the bed and putting his arm around her, he drew her close. 'Tell me, what did you dream about?'

Nithya squirmed in his grasp. His very touch seemed to fill her with loathing. But she could see that struggle was pointless.

'I dreamt that I was desperately running for my life in a jungle full of wild animals. I was exhausted by the time I reached the edge of the forest. I leaned against a tree, trying to catch my breath, and just when I thought I had made it, a great, big lion leaped in front of me, roaring. It was a huge relief to realize it was only a dream.'

Mukesh hardly heard a word she said. She looked so beautiful when she was agitated that he was mesmerized. 'You should have woken me up,' he said when he realized with a start that she had come to the end of her narrative.

She looked him straight in the eye. 'I would have, except when I heard you snoring, I realized where all the roaring animals in the dream came from,' she said mockingly, her smile not quite reaching her eyes.

Mukesh let go of her abruptly.

'Get ready,' he said, swinging his long legs off the bed. 'We have to go to the temple and later, we can have lunch at Saravana Bhavan.'

Nithya left the room feeling triumphant for having successfully drawn the boundaries to Mukesh. She never would let him get close to her! Her parents had bulldozed her into this marriage without pausing to consider her wishes. Well, if they thought they had won, it was time they had another think coming.

CHAPTER FIVE

After lunch at Saravana Bhavan, they went to the mall called Express Avenue for shopping. Mukesh spotted a pretty pink churidhar suit and asked, 'Do you like this outfit?'

'Oh yes ! it is very pretty,' she said. Then she noticed the price. 'This is very expensive. Let us look at something cheaper,' she said, moving on to the next rack.

'Don't worry about the cost,' Mukesh said, adding it to the shopping cart.

'Won't your mother feel hurt if we don't buy something for her? Let's buy her a saree.'

When she returned to the cash counter carrying two sarees instead of one, Mukesh looked at her in askance.

'This one's for your sister,' said Nithya, holding up one of the sarees. 'I like the churidhar suit very much. I think I'll wear it on my birthday.'

At the payment counter, Mukesh said, 'Now, can I pay for all this or do you want to take outfits for my nephews as well?'

Nithya looked at him doubtfully and seeing the crooked smile on his lips, realized that he was pulling her leg. 'That's up to you,' she said with a toss of her head, secretly gloating at the dent that she had made in his purse.

It was evening by the time they returned home after the shopping spree. Nithya showed her new outfit to her mother-in-law. As Lakshmi was admiring it, Nithya extracted a maroon saree from her bag and handed it to her.

'We bought this for you.'

Lakshmi gave a little crow of delight. 'Mukesh has never gotten me a saree,' she said, beaming from ear to ear. 'I am sure this is all thanks to my daughter-in-law,' she said and hugged Nithya.

The twilight was slowly dissolving into night when Lakshmi entered the kitchen to fix dinner.

Mukesh was sitting in the hall watching television when he saw Nithya approach him. She had freshened up and changed into a comfortable t-shirt and cotton pyjamas. She stood in front of Mukesh looking surreally beautiful and angelic. He looked at her and his breath caught in his throat. Standing there with her shoulder length hair hanging loose, she made for a stunning picture of youth and freshness.

He held her hand and gestured for her to sit by his side. Nithya, however, pulled herself away from him saying, "I cannot sit and watch TV like you. It wouldn't be proper for me to do so when my mother-in-law is slogging in the kitchen. I am going to help your mother in preparing dinner tonight."

Before Mukesh could retort, he saw his mother coming out of the kitchen, wiping her hands with a towel. Since the kitchen was adjoining to the hall, Lakshmi heard what Nithya had just said. Patting her daughter-in-law lovingly, she said, "there is no need for you to help me in preparing dinner. I have already finished and I am now going out to the temple along with Priya. Both of you can have dinner whenever you wish to."

Suddenly, Nithya's spirits dampened. She sat down on the sofa, far away from Mukesh. While Mukesh was watching cricket, she began fiddling with her mobile phone.

Mukesh decided he'd rather let her alone and continued watching the game. After half an hour, when there was a short commercial break, he switched off the television. "Come on Nithya, let's have dinner; I am really famished." He said and stood up.

Nithya followed him to the dinner table but continued playing the game in her cell phone.

Mukesh served her hot idlies and chutney and when he saw her devouring one idli after another, he said, "my mother is a great cook and no one can make soft idlies like she does."

Nithya nodded as she responded, "Really Superb, I have never eaten such soft idlies before!"

"Will you please put the cell phone down? No distractions while having food." Mukesh gently commanded.

Reluctantly, Nithya put away her cell phone and helped herself to more idlies and chutney. She relished her dinner silently without further conversation. Upon finishing her meal, she dropped her empty plate into the sink and rushed out with her cell phone - not caring to ask Mukesh if he wanted a second helping of idlies. Reclining on the bed, she continued playing the game from where she had left.

Half-an-hour later, Mukesh entered the bedroom. He bolted the door and sat down beside Nithya with the newspaper. Peering into her cell phone, he asked, "what is it you are so engrossed with since evening? Come on, let me have a look." He said as he placed a hand on her shoulder.

"Haven't you heard of candy crush saga? It is one of the most addictive puzzle games and whenever I feel bored it's what I play." Nithya said shoving his hand away from her shoulder.

Mukesh read the newspaper silently without speaking to her. Slowly, he got up from the bed and stifling a yawn, he said, "well Nithya...please stop your game. It is time for us to sleep now."

"Please...A few more minutes. This level is so interesting." She pleaded without looking up.

Mukesh relented. He waited patiently for a while and finally, grabbing the phone from her, said, "that's enough Nithya! You can continue tomorrow." He placed the cell phone on the table and was just about to turn off the lights, when Nithya squealed, "don't do that! I am afraid to sleep in the dark."

"That's not a problem for me. I can sleep when the lights are on." Mukesh said and once again went up to her. Sitting down beside her, he took her hand into his and toying with her fingers, said, "these little fingers must be really hurt playing sugar candy..."

"Candy crush not sugar candy." giggled Nithya.

"Oh, I see!" Mukesh said and slowly slid his hand into her T-Shirt.

Unhooking her bra in one swoop, he planted a deep kiss on her cheeks and said, "but right now, I am having a crush on you."

Slowly, Mukesh caressed her breasts. Nithya could feel her heart start to throb. She had to do something... she had to stop him from getting further. She saw the sly smile on his lips and decided that it was time to act. Now or never! She told herself. She would never let Mukesh come near her or consummate this marriage. She was all set to provoke him to the core, even to the point where he might become very wild and start hitting. It was her hope that She'd use it as a pretext to return to her parents' home. Why, she would plead with her father to even file a divorce for she could not continue living with a man who was a wife beater. All these she thought as Mukesh worked his bony fingers around her body.

Nithya had requested her parents to give her some more time. She believed that the man who had stolen her heart would, one day, return - he would come back for her. She had a feeling that something was holding him and had confidence that he would definitely come back to marry her. However, her parents were not willing to wait. They told her point blank that he was not the right man for her and forced her into the marriage with Mukesh. Nithya was determined to get back at her parents for not heeding to her request. She wished to do this by keeping herself far away from Mukesh, not letting him come close to her, and not consummate the marriage. For this, she was willing to take any risk in life.

She backed off from him suddenly and screamed, "have you lost your senses? What the hell is wrong with you?"

Mukesh was dumbfounded. "Why...nothing is wrong with me....I am just doing what all newly married couples do...."

Nithya decided to start a fight and she shouted, "Don't you have any manners ? Shouldn't you ask my permission ?"

"Oh! Since when do I have to seek permission to touch my legally wedded wife ?"

Nithya noticed that he was getting angry. Perhaps she could provoke him in to violence – that should give her grounds for a divorce. She said angrily, "So what if you are married to me ? First learn to be a gentleman. A gentleman would first make sure that his wife is willing for intimacies and not just force himself on her."

Nithya huffed and when Mukesh held her close once again, she said, "now...please don't touch me...I am in no mood for this. Just go and sleep and let me play with my cell phone."

"Nithya, please stop acting like an unruly child! Just don't create a scene...O.K.?" Mukesh said softly.

Nithya, hellbent on making him angry, shouted at the top of her voice, "will you please leave me alone!"

Mukesh stared at her in silence as she continued, "why are you looking at me like that? Are you going to hit me or something?"

Mukesh only continued to stare at her, all the while wondering the reason for such huffy behavior. "If you continue to behave like an unruly child, I am left with no option but to beat you," he said tongue-in-cheek.

This was the window of opportunity Nithya had been hoping for, she ran to the door and started banging it with all her might. "How dare you say that?"

Mukesh followed her almost instantly and held her hands firmly and said, "why all this drama Nithya ?" While Nithya started wrestling with him, he heard someone knock the door from outside.

Letting Nithya go, he opened the door. His mother stood outside. 'Is something wrong?' she asked anxiously.

Mukesh turned red and stuttered, 'It's nothing, Ma ... actually we were ...'

But Nithya was sobbing inside the room. His mother did not need any further explanation. She said, 'Be kind and understanding towards her. She is just a child.'

Before he could say anything, she turned and walked away. Mukesh shut the door and returned to the bed. Nithya was weeping into her pillow. He stood for a few minutes just watching her body wracked with sobs. He sat on the bed beside her and patted her back and said, "well, I have decided not to disturb you tonight. Now, please stop crying."

After he turned off the light, he lay in bed staring into the dark for a long time, deeply troubled. Why was she behaving in this manner? What exactly was in her mind? As a child, he had never been able to understand his mother. And now, he couldn't understand his wife. To fathom the depths of the ocean would be easier than understanding the workings of a woman's mind. His last thought as he finally dozed off was that he'd need to somehow find a way to win her trust.

CHAPTER SIX

It was 6.00 a.m. in the morning when Mukesh woke up. He saw that Nithya was still asleep. He heard the clatter of pots and pans in the kitchen. His mother was up and he stood up to go and join her. The aroma of freshly brewed coffee hit him square as he walked into the kitchen.

Lakshmi glanced at him before proceeding to set a cup of coffee on the table for him. 'Your sister is leaving for Coimbatore today as the children's school is reopening shortly. I will be accompanying her this time.'

'Ma, how can you leave me in the lurch like this?' Mukesh asked in despair.

'I am not leaving you alone, Mukesh. Now you have your wife to take care of you,' she said.

'But I don't think she will ever take care of me!"

'Please, Mukesh, try to be more understanding..."

Clearly trying to disguise his annoyance, he replied his mother through gritted teeth, 'stop talking about your wonderful daughter-in-law, Ma, and give me something to eat, I'm starving!'

Rolling out the chappatis, Lakshmi said, "She is in your life for a special reason, so please adjust with her..."

Mukesh bent his head and raked his fingers through his hair, 'Please, Ma, don't lecture me.'

'But this is very important. It concerns your life!' She paused to calm herself and placed the plate of chappatis and kurma on the table in front of Mukesh, before continuing in an even tone, 'Look, son, don't expect everything to be picture perfect. Both of you are only human after all. You are made differently and there will naturally be differences of opinions; but married life is full of small misunderstandings, reconciliations, and compromises. This, in fact, strengthens the bond between husband and wife.'

'Ma, don't talk rubbish!' said Mukesh in exasperation. 'I'm not a saint or a martyr or a block of wood like you!'

Lakshmi was stunned by his sharp words. "You seem to be in a really bad mood ..."

Mukesh bit back a retort. As a child, he had often noticed his mother crying quietly. At the time, he had vowed to make things right and had sworn that when he grew up he would ensure that his mother was always happy and smiling.

CHAPTER SEVEN

Mukesh knew his mother never had a bad word for anybody. According to her, goodness was inherent in the human race and people's misdemeanours were usually attributable to their circumstances.

Mukesh was in high school when his mother's classmate and close friend, Radhika, moved into the neighbourhood. Radhika came to meet her every day and both of them did their shopping together. On weekends, she'd accompany Lakshmi's family on outings. Very soon, Radhika became close to Mukesh's father as well.

After a few months, however, Radhika's visits grew less frequent, although she telephoned every morning. After speaking to Lakshmi for a few minutes, she would ask to speak to her husband. Lakshmi would trustingly hand the phone over to her husband and carry on with her household chores.

Radhika's friendship with Mukesh's father soon turned into an illicit love affair and she spoke to him on his cell phone every morning. Lakshmi noticed that her husband was full of smiles whenever he spoke to Radhika. She didn't object to their conversations, for she trusted her husband implicitly. It was only when she noticed her husband going out to the balcony for privacy every time Radhika called him that her alarm bells went off. Out of sheer curiosity one morning, Lakshmi eavesdropped on their conversation.

'Please, Radhika, try to understand. I can't live without you ... I am deeply in love with you ...'

Lakshmi felt her world collapse around her. She was devastated and feeling blatantly betrayed by the two people closest to her, she wept in rage and sorrow.

Her husband emerged from his bath and stopped short on noticing his wife's red and puffy eyes, 'What's the matter?'

'Stop it! Don't pretend to be a caring husband! 'How dare you do this to me? Are you out of your mind! Radhika...that bitch may not care about ruining my life, but what the hell is wrong with you?'

'Lakshmi, please ... stop crying. Let me explain everything to you. I would never leave you. I never intended to hide anything from you ...but I didn't know how to tell you.'

Holding both her hands, he begged like a child, 'Lakshmi, I don't know what has come over me...but I have fallen madly in love with her. Lakshmi, I confess I love Radhika. But I don't want to hurt you and I can't bear to see you so miserable. Please, Lakshmi, tell me what to do...I didn't fall in love on purpose, it just happened. Now, where do we go from here?

Lakshmi was stunned. Her husband of eighteen years had betrayed the trust she had on him!

Shaking with anger, Lakshmi stalked out of the room. As the great bard once said: 'hell hath no fury like a woman scorn'd' —Lakshmi decided to confront Radhika.

Although Radhika was taken aback by the sudden visit, she invited Lakshmi in with a smile.

Lakshmi came straight to the point. 'Radhika, you have deceived me in the worst possible way.'

Radhika said, 'Lakshmi, it was not my fault. Sometimes, things go beyond our control. I don't know how to explain this to you...Your husband ...'

'I don't give a damn, Radhika! You can – and have to – put an end to this nonsense.'

'Lakshmi, please, please, try to understand my position. I am really helpless in this matter. It was your husband who started it and he is so deeply in love with me and says he cannot live without me.'

Radhika's puerile justification got on Lakshmi's nerves and she snapped, 'Oh, shut up Radhika! This cannot go on. I will report your behaviour to your husband, and let's see what he has to say about it!'

Hearing the raised voices, Radhika's husband came down to the drawing room looking questioningly at the two women. Radhika left the room without a word.

Lakshmi told him everything, leaving nothing out. 'Please ask your wife not to ruin my life.'

'Madam,' said the gentleman, apologetically, 'I am indeed aware of everything. I can understand your anxiety and worry because I am in the same boat. She is a willful and stubborn woman and I am unable to change her mind. She threatens to divorce me if I get in her way.'

After a moment of silence, he continued, 'she is such a pig-headed woman and I am afraid she might end her life if I threaten or hit her. Thinking of my two children who will then become motherless, I finally decided not to interfere in her affairs.'

Dumbstruck, Lakshmi left Radhika's strange household without another word. By the time she returned home, she had arrived at a momentous decision. For the sake of her children, who loved their father, she decided to forgive her erring husband. Furthermore, without her husband's financial support, she didn't know how she would be able to manage things at home. She didn't fancy living on hand-outs and the goodwill of friends and relatives.

Lakshmi slowly accepted her destiny and adjusted herself. On week-ends, when her husband returned home late or worst did not turn up in the night, she understood that he was having a jolly time with her friend. On such occasions, she couldn't stem the flow of her tears and wept over the cruel blow that fate had dealt her. Two years later, her husband passed away in a road accident.

Mukesh had been by her side like a rock with his steadfast support all through the darkest days of her life.

Ever since then, Mukesh had been an archetypal son, sensitive to his mother's feelings; her every wish was his command.

CHAPTER EIGHT

After she was packed and ready to leave for Coimbatore, Lakshmi looked for Mukesh. She found him on the swing seat in the veranda, moodily swaying to and fro. 'If you need anything at all, my dear, you are most welcome to call me at any time. I'll always have my phone with me.'

Mukesh said nothing. He couldn't help worrying that without his mother's reassuring presence, more issues would crop up. He sensed that there was something bothering Nithya. However, he did not want to probe deeper. It was best to give her some space.

It was almost noon when Nithya went to the kitchen to make lunch. Mukesh had not spoken to her since morning. Perhaps he was still in a huff over her last night's drama. This was exactly what she wanted. She was feeling triumphant that her plan was working. To her surprise she found Mukesh in the kitchen, dicing tomatoes.

'Can I help with the cooking?' she asked.

Mukesh ignored her, so Nithya repeated, 'Can I help you?'

Mukesh said curtly, 'My mother has taught me to cook, so I don't need anybody's help.'

He was really cut up with her, she thought, silently patting herself on the back. She sat down at the glass dining table in the kitchen and watched him cook. When he was done, he went into the living room and sat down on a couch with his laptop. Nithya plopped down beside him. His silence was a bit unnerving, so she turned on the television. She surfed until she found a music channel and turned up the volume, observing him all the while from the corner of her eye.

His face deadpan, he continued to be deeply engrossed in his work. After a while, he shut his laptop and went off to have his lunch in solitary splendor.

Nithya continued to watch television, expecting him to call her. When he didn't, Nithya decided to starve rather than join him for lunch uninvited.

After some time, she switched off the television, lay back on the couch and fell asleep. It was late in the evening when she woke up. She was famished. She walked into the kitchen looking for something to eat. The food that Mukesh had made was on the counter, but she did not touch it. Instead, she ate the stale chapattis leftover from breakfast.

It was nearing bed time and Nithya was getting panicky. Last night Mukesh had threatened her with a beating if she refused to cooperate with him. He had also been giving her the silent treatment since this morning which confirmed the fact that he was angry with her over last night's episode. She slowly walked into the bedroom feeling like a lamb to the slaughter.

Mukesh was half-reclined on the bed with his laptop. He looked up at her but did not react to her presence. Unable to bear the silence any longer she decided to take the bull by the horns.

She moved closer to the bed and stood there with her hands on her hips, glowering at him. Mukesh continued to be engrossed in his work and barely noticed her. In a frenzy, she ripped off her T-shirt and flung it at his face, shrieking, 'Now, come and have your fill! Isn't this is what you want? You are a sex maniac. Come and rape me and satisfy all your sexual appetite.' Nithya then burst into tears.

Oh, God! Not again, thought Mukesh as he closed his laptop and stood up, wondering how he was going to subdue her.

The previous night, Mukesh had been dreadfully embarrassed when his mother had hurried to their room upon hearing the commotion in the bedroom. She had also advised him to treat his wife kindly and offended by this, Mukesh had decided to leave her alone. The last thing he wanted now was a fresh argument and upheavals even before their married life had taken off; therefore, he opted for the ostrich-with-its-head-in-the-sand approach and had immersed himself in his office work and avoid any confrontation.

In one fluid movement, Mukesh picked up the T-shirt and slipped it over his truculent wife's head. 'Now tell me,' he said, 'why this drama?'

In response, Nithya was determined to rile and provoke him further, 'You don't seem to care about me. Or is your office work more important to you than me?' 'Hope you are not angry with me over last night's behavior. You haven't even spoken a word to me since morning!'

Mukesh gently wiped her tears and sat her on the bed. He gestured to the screen of his laptop and said, 'Look at the number of emails I have received. I was only catching up with work stuff. Besides, whenever I come near you, you become so tense and agitated. I thought it best to maintain my distance and give you some time to settle down.'

She continued to sob disconsolately. 'Nithya, please don't throw these tantrums and make my life miserable. Be frank and share your problems with me. Tell me exactly what it is you want I'll try to fulfil your wishes – whatever they are!"

This was definitely opportunity knocking and Nithya decided to make the most of it.

Tears forgotten, Nithya pouted and said, 'Actually ... I had great ambitions in life ... I wanted to continue my studies ... do my MBA ... and then get a job. But my parents hastily arranged my marriage ...'

With a gentle pat on her shoulder, Mukesh said, 'That isn't a problem at all. You should have told me about it before. It is not too late even now. I shall arrange for your admission in a reputed college and you can continue with your MBA. And, I promise to behave like a perfect gentleman and not touch you until you want me to. Is that okay?'

Sniffing and wiping away her tears, Nithya smiled her thanks.

It was strangely touching that he had complied to her request without putting up any resistance – something that her own father had failed to do. Her parents had gotten rid of her like yesterday's garbage. Her anger boiled over again at that thought. They would regret their actions for the rest of their lives!

Mukesh had gullibly believed every word she had told him. This would enable her to keep him at arm's length for a while longer...

CHAPTER NINE

Returning from the office one evening, Mukesh opened the vault in the closet. That was when he noticed with a sense of shock that Nithya had removed her mangalsutra, toe-rings and had placed them beside the cashbox. Mukesh knew that most Indian women were emotionally attached to these symbols of wedlock which represented love, trust and marital happiness. They would never be seen without these pieces of jewellery.

'Nithya!'

When Nithya hurried into the room and saw him standing by the open closet, she realized why he had summoned her and turned tail to retreat. Mukesh, however, was quick to grab her hand. He pulled her to the cashbox and indicated the offending items with a wave of his hand. 'What's all this? Are you going to college without these?'

'Yes.'

'With whose permission did you take them off? Shouldn't you discuss it with me before taking such a drastic decision?' he asked softly, keeping a tight rein on his temper.

'Do I have to ask your permission for each and every thing? Don't I have the freedom to do whatever I please?' she demanded.

'Nithya, you can't be so naïve. Aren't you aware that, in our society, only a widow and an unmarried woman has no mangalsutra?'

Nithya was secretly delighted to see that she had finally succeeded in needling him. Mukesh was still lecturing her, 'These are not mere trinkets for you to discard on a whim. They are sacred symbols of wedlock and –'

Nithya interrupted him, 'see, you have said it yourself. They are mere symbols of marriage. What matters is the bond between the couple in a marital relationship. There are many hypocrites who flaunt these marital symbols even as they flout their vows and happily cheat on their spouses. Marriage isn't just about flaunting symbols, is it, Mukesh?'

Mukesh appreciated her point of view; however, he said, 'What will people say if they –'

Not letting him air his opinion, Nithya said, 'The value of these "symbols" has diminished nowadays. The decision to wear them or not is ours to make. Why bother about what others think, do or say?'

'Well, in that case, it is my decision that you should not go out without these. Come on, put them on,' he commanded.

Nithya shook her head. 'No. I don't want to wear them to college.'

Thoroughly riled by now, Mukesh mounted his high horse and said, 'Nithya, you are acting like someone who has lived all her life in America. Remember, you are in India, the land which gives great importance to traditional and cultural practices. There was a time when Indian women didn't hesitate to immolate themselves on their husbands' pyres. How come you are so different from the rest of them?

Nithya was also fully into character by now and taking his hands into hers, she said, 'Be a little practical and try to understand my feelings too! I am surrounded by unmarried girls and boys, talking about careers and further studies abroad. I feel inferior in their midst. I do not want them to know that I am married, lest I become the butt of their jokes. Please permit me to go without these to the college ... please ... please ... please ...'

He was silent and, seeing the hesitation on his face, Nithya conceded, 'Okay ... I'll wear them at home. But at least let me go to the college without them.' She pleaded like a child and Mukesh found himself relenting.

'Okay, Nithya, do as you please,' he said and walked away.

Nithya heaved a sigh of relief. For once, she had been able to arrive at a compromise by simply speaking the truth – nothing but the truth. What was the point of flaunting these symbols of marriage when, all the while, you were cheating on your spouse?

CHAPTER TEN

Pavithra was on tenterhooks as she waited for her best friend in the lecture hall. Was she having trouble on the home front again? Pavithra was still dithering about going in search of her, when she saw Nithya enter the class room. As Pavithra waved her over, she thought to herself that this girl needed some serious counselling and decided it was high time they had a little heart-to-heart with Nithya – today, during the lunch break, perhaps.

The previous evening, after classes had concluded, Mukesh had been waiting at the college gates for Nithya. Nithya, clearly embarrassed, had introduced him as her cousin. Pavithra, the only one among their friends who knew the truth, could sense Mukesh's discomfort with the lie, but Mukesh had said nothing and merely smiled before leading Nithya to his car.

During the first few days in college, Pavithra had been drawn to Nithya by the fact that, like her, Nithya was also married. However, unlike Nithya, Pavithra had no wish to hide her marital status and wore her mangalsutra and toe-rings with pride. Nithya had revealed her personal story to her and Pavithra knew how Nithya despised her parents for forcing her into this marriage. College, to Nithya, was merely a means of keeping her husband at bay.

Even so, Pavithra felt Nithya had crossed the line when she introduced her husband as her cousin.

During their lunch break in the canteen, Pavithra said, 'Don't you think you are being very unfair to your husband?'

'What do you mean?' Nithya said affronted.

'Stop playing the innocent. You know exactly what I mean. Isn't it very unkind of you to introduce your husband as a cousin? I was surprised he wasn't offended with you.'

'Oh, he doesn't mind. I have told him I didn't want people in college to know that I'm married,' Nithya said, nonchalantly.

Clearly annoyed now, Pavithra said, "That doesn't mean that you can disown your husband whenever you like for no fault of his.'

'Come on Pavithra, what do you want me to do?' snapped Nithya.

'You need to forgive your parents and move on with your life. You cannot ruin your present by clinging to the past,' Pavithra said softly.

Nithya was furious now, 'Pavithra, it is easier to preach than to practise. Step into my shoes and you'll understand my anguish.'

Pavithra was offended by her unwarranted rudeness. 'Nithya, no one can understand you better than I do. I know how it is when your own parents do not trust you ... do not believe a word you say ... and betray you. In fact, we are both in the same boat.'

As Nithya looked at her uncomprehendingly, Pavithra narrated her story.

It had happened a few months after Pavithra joined college. In school, she had had an active role in extra-curricular activities and school functions. A good writer, she had regularly contributed to her school magazine as well. In college, she had continued her activities with the same zeal. One fine day, a circular on the college notice board inviting contributions for the college magazine caught her eye. Delighted at the opportunity, Pavithra got down to work with her usual enthusiasm. Burning the midnight oil, she wrote five poems on the theme of love. Then, exhausted, she left them on her desk and went to bed ...

Her maternal aunt who had been staying with them was due to leave the next day. She had stayed up late to pack her things and, just before going to bed, she had peeked into her niece's room to see if she was awake. It was then that her eyes fell on the papers scattered on the study table. She started to stack them neatly, admiring Pavithra's beautiful handwriting. Before placing a paper weight on them, she casually read a few lines and was appalled.

The next morning, before leaving, she poisoned her sister's mind. 'Just look at what your pampering and leniency has led to! Pavithra has fallen in love with some boy and has been spending her nights writing love poems to him. If you don't take drastic action now, the consequences will be dire. Who knows? She could even elope with him one fine day bringing you shame and disgrace.'

That evening, when Pavithra returned from college, her parents interrogated her at length. Although Pavithra did her best to convince them that those poems were written for her college magazine, her explanations fell on deaf ears. Her father decided to pull her out of college and arranged to get her married immediately.

Luckily for her, her husband turned out to be a generous and kind-hearted man and, when he heard her tale, he promised to send her to college to pursue her studies and also agreed to postpone having children until she was ready to start a family.

Pavithra confided in Nithya, 'I also harbored hatred towards my parents for a long time. But, with time, I was able to forgive them. Nithya, I'm telling you this so that you can liberate yourself as well from the clutches of hatred and move on. It is high time you started leading a happy life with your husband instead of being at loggerheads with him to spite your parents.'

Nithya, too stunned to respond, only nodded.

Pavithra hugged Nithya impulsively, 'I am sure you will Nithya. God does not give us challenges we cannot conquer. He knows our limits and is only putting us to the test.'

Nithya looked at her in silence. Pavithra, my dear friend, that is easier said than done, she thought.

CHAPTER ELEVEN

Nithya found it difficult to concentrate on her studies or focus on anything for that matter. Each day, a new crisis cropped up and she was having a tough time coping.

And now, this: she had failed her semester exams and the lady Proctor had asked to meet her parents. Nithya had informed her that she was married and that her husband was now her official guardian. However, she followed this up by lying that her husband was out of town and could not come for the meeting. As a special case, the Proctor gave her all the test papers and report card and asked Nithya to get them signed on her husband's return.

Nithya was not sure how Mukesh would react when it came to her low marks. She sat at the dining table, nibbling on a vegetable sandwich, pondering the issue, when she had a brainwave.

She rummaged through the papers on the desk in his study and found a receipt with his signature on it. After several abortive attempts on a notepaper, she managed a passably good forgery of his signature. When the doorbell rang, she quickly hid the sheet and receipt under a large dictionary on the desk and went to answer the door.

It was Mukesh. She smiled briefly at him before escaping to the kitchen.

Handing him his coffee, she said perfunctorily, 'I have to study. There's a test tomorrow,' and abruptly left the room.

Long after Mukesh had gone to bed that night, she crept down the stairs and placed her test papers and report card under his laptop.

She tossed and turned all night long wondering how Mukesh would react when he saw the critical remarks of the principal. She felt a twinge of conscience, but determinedly squelched the guilt. She had no feelings for him. Why should she care what he thought?

The next morning, at breakfast, she braced herself for a dressing down, but Mukesh didn't raise the issue. He continued to eat his breakfast, his usual circumspect self.

Finally, she could stand it no longer. As he bent over to lace his shoes, she confronted him hands on her hips, 'Did you see those papers?'

'What papers?' he said, not looking up.

'The ones I had placed under your laptop,' she said, irked by his lackadaisical attitude. 'My test papers and report card!'

'Oh, those! I thought they were for framing and displaying in a museum!' he said rather matter-of-factly.

Nithya managed to keep a straight face with difficulty as she fought down an urge to laugh out loud at his sarcasm. She was pleasantly surprised at Mukesh's light-hearted approach to the matter. However, she became cross when he continued, 'I am not going to sign those papers. You may take them back.'

Go to hell, she cursed under her breath, and flounced out of the room.

She grabbed the papers and report card and marched down the steps. Once inside the car, she fumbled for her pen to sign the papers herself. To her surprise, she saw that Mukesh had already signed them. She checked all the test papers one by one and in the end her heart skipped several beats when she saw the sheet of paper on which she had practised forging his signature. She had forgotten to tear it up. She wanted to kick herself for such carelessness.

Mukesh locked the house and slowly walked to the car. Nithya did not dare look at him. She was silent throughout the journey. Finally, when he stopped in front of campus gates, she said, 'I'm sorry.'

'It's okay,' he said with a smile. 'I hope you do better next time. After all, practice makes perfect, doesn't it? But you know that already, for you were spot on with my signature.'

He was pulling her leg and admonishing her at the same time, damn it! She slammed the car door and walked off without responding to him.

CHAPTER TWELVE

Nithya frantically rummaged through her bag for her cell phone. It was 4 p.m. and time for Mukesh's call. On the days that he got stuck at work and couldn't pick her up, as soon as she returned from college, Mukesh would speak to her for a few minutes just to make sure she had reached home safely. The conversation invariably took a standard tack:

'How was your day in college?'

'Okay.'

'How was lunch?'

'Good.'

The phone rang almost as soon as she took it out. However, it wasn't Mukesh, but an unidentified number. Nithya hesitated a moment, then took the call.

'Hello?' she said.

There was no response.

'Hello?' she repeated. 'Who's this?'

'Hello, Nithya.'

The voice! She recognized it at once. For a moment, she could not breathe.

'Giridhar!' she breathed.

'I have missed you, Nithya.'

'Giridhar, where were you all these days? I have tried and tried to contact you, but your phone was ...'

Giridhar cut her off gently by saying, 'Nithya, let me explain. Both my sisters passed away in a horrific accident and my mother hasn't recovered from the shock as yet.'

'Oh no! I'm so very sorry!'

Nithya was at a loss for words but managed to stammer out sadly, 'Two whole months, Giridhar ... you had switched off your phone! Who does that ...'

Giridhar immediately interrupted her, 'Mum clings to me like a child. She is not willing to send me back to Chennai. Mother had hid the cell phone in the bureau and after searching for it continuously for two days, I gave up. I was not able to contact anybody. She was upset that the owner of the Pizza shop in Chennai where I used to work was phoning up to me everyday insisting that I return to work soon. On the other hand, my mother was not willing to let me go out anywhere. Only yesterday, I confessed to her about our love affair and she has agreed to our marriage. Hence I have come down to Chennai to meet your parents and discuss about our marriage...'

Nithya stopped him suddenly. 'But Giridhar... how am I to know about your predicament. So much has happened that I don't know where to start. Immediately after my graduation, my parents decided to get me married. I protested and told them about you. They wanted to meet you ... and I frantically tried to contact you ... but your cell phone was switched off.

Finally, I had no other option ... but to give in to them and get married to the person they chose for me.'

There was a long moment of silence, in which Nithya could only hear his raspy breathing.

'Giridhar, speak to me,' she pleaded. 'It wasn't my fault. There was nothing I could do.'

'I don't blame you, Nithya.' His voice was thick with sorrow. 'It is my own bloody luck. I have lost everything I hold dear.'

After another long pause, he said, 'Nithya, can I ask you something? You don't have to answer if you don't want to. But you sound sad. Are you happy in your marriage?'

Nithya remained silent, unsure of what to say.

At her silence, Giridhar said forcefully, 'Nithya, be frank with me. Your happiness means everything to me. An unhappy marriage need not come between us ...'

It was this whole-hearted expression of his feelings that had made her fall head-over-heels in love with him in the first place.

'Giridhar, your words mean so much to me. Talking to you is a great solace, but just think of what You're saying. I am a married woman now ...'

'No, Nithya, please don't misunderstand me. What I am trying to say is that, if you are not happy with this marriage, you can divorce him and come to me. I am still here for you and shall be willing to receive you with open arms.'

Nithya hesitated, then spoke softly, 'I do miss you a lot, Giridhar ...'

On hearing that, Giridhar seemed to abandon all attempts at self-restraint. 'Nithya, tell me when can I come and see you?'

CHAPTER THIRTEEN

Nithya's childhood had been an easy one. Her workaholic parents provided her with every luxury. If there was anything that was lacking, it was their time and attention.

Nithya's mother had no time to be a homemaker. However, despite her busy schedule, she managed to provide a light breakfast of toast or cornflakes every morning. The family of three quite often lunched and dined in restaurants or on takeaways. With the pocket money that her parents gave her, Nithya could order food of her choice every day.

Nithya learned early to bottle up her emotions and not share her problems with anyone because her parents were either busy at work, tired after work, working late or even working from home. As a child, when she had been bursting with news about her day, they would cut her off, saying, 'Please, darling, give me some time to change my clothes. I will join you shortly.'

They never did 'join her shortly' although Nithya would eagerly wait for them. The child would go back to her room feeling dejected and alone. However, she adapted, as children are wont to do, and led a sequestered existence.

It was during her second year in college that her life suddenly transformed. One evening, she returned home from college, famished. It was only 3.30 p.m. and she decided to order a pizza. Half an hour later, when the doorbell rang, all thoughts of pizza fled. The handsome pizza delivery boy was every teenage girl's fantasy. He had really black hair, square shaped face and well chiseled chin. She immediately fell for his strong muscular arms and unusually deeply matured voice given his age.

Nithya ordered pizza every day just to see him but couldn't actually work up the courage to speak to him.

One evening, however, he said in his deep voice, 'Ma'am, can I have some water, please?'

When Nithya handed him the glass of water, he said, 'Thank you, ma'am. This Chennai heat is so unbearable that I'm parched.'

Nithya smiled in response but said nothing.

Returning the glass to her, he asked with concern in his voice, 'is your mother also working? I have not seen her even once.'

Nithya soon found herself talking to him and telling him confidingly, 'Yeah! both my parents are working and they work late.'

'Poor little rich girl!' he chuckled. 'Born with the proverbial silver spoon but ordering pizza every day.'

Nithya laughed.

On a sudden whim, Nithya invited him to share her pizza, which he graciously accepted.

As they ate, he told her about himself. 'My name is Giridhar and I'm originally from Rajasthan. I had to abandon my studies when my father passed away last year, to support my family and educate my two younger sisters. I came to Chennai along with my neighbor who was already settled in Chennai. He promised to find a nice job for me here. I am now working in a Pizza shop as a delivery boy. However, I am also learning the basics of running a pizza center at present and I plan to open one of my own very soon.'

When he saw that Nithya had almost finished her pizza, he stood up and said, 'I've gotta go now. Uh ... shall I wait for the payment or collect it tomorrow?'

Nithya slapped her forehead. 'Oh, my God! Haven't I paid you yet? I clean forgot!' She hurried away to get the money.

After he'd left, she realized something with sudden clarity – Giridhar had stolen her heart!

CHAPTER FOURTEEN

Giridhar visited her every evening. Their friendship blossomed over time. Nithya soon found herself opening up to him in a way she rarely did with others.

'My parents are always busy in the office and I feel so lonely in life! If only I had a sibling like my other friends!'

'But you have me now,' he said, smiling. 'I'll take care of you ... always.'

'I know, Giridhar, you will always be there for me. Can I tell you about an incident that happened quite some time ago?'

'Go on, then ... I am all ears,' he said.

'I was ill in school one day and sent home because I was running a temperature. My father was away on business that day, so I telephoned my mother. But she was in meetings all day, so she sent me to the hospital with the maid. I was diagnosed with malarial fever and was bedridden for almost a week. My mother did not bother to take leave to tend to me and there I was, alone at home, with a pile of bitter medicines. I often wonder why they even gave birth to me.'

Giridhar listened, then said, 'But you must understand one thing, Nithya, they are, after all, working so hard to give you a luxurious life. Isn't money the elixir of life?'

Nithya pouted. 'But money alone isn't enough. Sometimes we crave attention and a human touch. If my mother had given me those quinine pills herself, it would have made a huge difference, don't you think so? And my father? Two months ago, he presented me with a Scooty on my birthday. He promised to teach me to ride it over the weekend. That weekend is yet to come.'

'If you are willing, I can teach you. I assure you that within an hour, you will be able to ride the Scooty on your own,' Giridhar offered.

'Can we start tomorrow?' Nithya asked, excited.

'Sure, why not?' Giridhar said, laughing.

The next day, a Saturday, was Giridhar's day off. He arrived at 10 a.m. and they went to a secluded playground. With Giridhar's guidance, Nithya learned quickly. By noon, she was confidently taking the Scooty around the yard, with Giridhar riding pillion.

Happily, she told him, 'Now, get off. I'll do the next round without your help.' Giridhar obliged and sat down on a rock by the side of the path.

This was her first solo ride and Nithya rode slowly and carefully. But then she began daydreaming about her father's delight when he sees her prowess on the two-wheeler. A small puddle was her undoing when, trying to manoeuvre around it at the last minute, she tipped over and fell with an ignominious splash.

'Oh my god, Nithya! Are you okay?' Giridhar asked as he ran to help her up.

He gingerly lifted the Scooty off the young girl and helped her to her feet. With an arm around her, he helped her limp to the large boulder by the path so she could sit down. She was bleeding from a cut on her foot, but otherwise seemed to have come off lightly.

'You've hurt yourself,' scolded Giridhar as he extracted the first-aid kit from the Scooty's dickey under the seat. It was brand new and he broke the seal. Using a cotton swab soaked in the disinfectant that was also provided in the kit, he gently tended to the cut.

Nithya winced but did not protest. Giridhar taped a band aid over the cleaned cut and rose to his feet. Smiling encouragingly, he said, 'that's enough for today. You are already an ace rider. Time to go home.' He jerked his head indicating to her to hop on behind him.

What had started out as riding lessons, evolved into a routine. Every Saturday, Giridhar came by to pick her up and they went to the beach or a nearby park or a mall and spent the day enjoying each other's company.

Nithya always looked forward to these outings.

After a shopping spree one sunny afternoon, Nithya said, 'If only we could stay together always ... until the end of our lives ...' she sighed, dreamily.

'How is that even possible?' said Giridhar with shake of his handsome head. 'You will soon finish your graduation and get busy with a job. You will have no more time for me ...'

Nithya interrupted him, 'Don't say such things. I don't think I could go a single day without you. You are the only one in this whole wide world who has any time for me. You are the one who showed me a world beyond the four walls of my house and brought me out of my shell ... took me places ... and opened my eyes. Giridhar, I want you by my side like this for all eternity.'

Giridhar smiled at her and said, 'Nithya, to tell you the truth, I too feel the same way.'

'Actually ...' Nithya started hesitantly before her courage failed her. Taking a deep breath, she started again, saying in a low voice, 'if you are willing ... I can talk to my parents ... and we can get married and ...'

Giridhar burst out laughing and said, 'Please, Nithya, stop joking. It would never work out ... we belong to different castes and regions and our social status is also very different ...'

Offended by his attitude, Nithya interrupted him sharply, 'Don't you know that true love knows no barriers? They are merely man-made while our love is sacred and has happened spontaneously ... I am sure I can convince my parents ... after all, they've dedicated their lives to my happiness. If I tell them about my love, I am sure they will not object or ...'

Giridhar laughed again. 'Nithya, grow up! You belong to a rich family. Your parents are probably dreaming of getting you married to a rich guy with a great big bungalow, a Mercedez Benz and a million servants at your beck and call. How do you think they'll react when you tell them that you wish to marry a pizza delivery boy?'

Nithya, upset at his cavalier attitude to her proposal, rebuked him sharply, 'stop laughing. I am serious about this. For a happy married life, it is not money or riches that is important. It is the heart which really matters! When I confess to my parents about my love for you, I am sure they will understand.'

'Well Nithya, if you really mean that, then, first I must become worthy to meet your parents.'

The next evening after Nithya returned from college, she was delighted to see Giridhar waiting for her by the gate.

Giridhar, however, did not return her smile.

'Something wrong?' she asked, concerned. 'What's the matter? Come on in, talk to me.'

Giridhar grimaced and said, 'I've been running from pillar to post trying to get a bank loan to set up my pizza center. This morning, the bank manager called me and said that unless I produce some collateral security they won't sanction my loan. He sighed and looked away. 'If your parents ever agree to see me, I want to present myself as the owner of a pizza shop, not a pizza delivery boy. I don't know whom to ask for a loan ...'

Nithya thought for a minute and said, 'I may be able to help ... can you wait a minute?'

She returned a few minutes later with a small wooden box containing gold ornaments. Handing it to him, she said, 'This is the jewellery my parents have bought for my marriage. There is more than a kilo of gold in here. You can use it as security against the loan.'

Giridhar looked shocked. 'Are you mad?' he uttered incredulously. 'How could you think that I would accept this from you? That too, without your parents' permission!' And instantly shoved the box back into her hands.

'Don't make such a fuss. Isn't it my responsibility to help my future husband?'

But Giridhar dug his heels in. 'I have a few friends who may be willing to help. I'll figure something out.'

Nithya placed her hand on his arm to hold him back. 'Giridhar, I insist you take this jewellery. I don't want you to be beholden to “some friend. Moreover, this is just a loan. You could always return the jewels when the pizza outlet breaks even.’

Shoving the jewel box into his hands, she said, ‘If you love me at all, do not refuse!’

Reluctantly, Giridhar took the box from her. ‘You have now put me in a very embarrassing situation, Nithya. You know I love you so much! Thanks, Nithya...I don’t know what to say. Well...Thanks a lot Nithya.’

Giridhar suddenly became emotional and speechless and seeing him struggle for words, Nithya said, ‘come on Giridhar, don’t get so emotional. You don’t have to keep thanking me. It is after-all for your business that I am giving all this.

The next day, Nithya waited anxiously to find out whether his loan had been approved. But when Giridhar did not show up at his usual time, she became restless. Couldn’t he at least call, she thought, annoyed.

It was at around 8 p.m., a few minutes before her parents’ arrival that she decided to call him. To her shock, his phone was switched off!

Her attempts to contact him the following day were also futile. Every day, immediately after returning from college, she tried his number over and over again. Finally, she gave up!

CHAPTER FIFTEEN

It was Parvathi's wedding anniversary and she was getting ready to go to the temple. She opened the vault to take out her diamond necklace but, to her horror, the jewellery case was missing. She frantically scrabbled around every nook and corner of the safe ... but the box was gone.

'Nithya!' she called, anxiously. 'Did you take the jewellery box from here?'

'Yes, Ma, I took it. I loaned the jewellery to a friend.'

'A friend? What friend?'

'His name is Giridhar.'

'A boy? How long have you known him? Is he from your college?'

'No, Ma, I met him a few months ago and we have been going out together.'

This was going from bad to worse. Parvathi was staggered. 'I don't believe this! Met him? Where? How? Oh my god, how long has this nonsense been going on?'

Nithya's eyes filled with tears.

'How could you be so foolish, Nithya? Meeting a loafer off the street behind our backs! And going so far as to give your jewellery to him!'

'Ma, please don't be angry and try to understand me. He is not a loafer. He is the only person in this world who has any time for me. I feel wanted when I am with him. He is planning to set up a pizza center of his own and trying to obtain a loan for this enterprise from different banks. He did not ask me for any financial help; It was I who insisted he take the jewels as collateral for the loan –'

'And it never occurred to you to tell us about any of this?' Parvathi interrupted her impatiently.

'It was not my intention to hide anything from you, Ma. I was only waiting for an opportune moment to talk to you about this, but you were always so busy with your office work that I kept procrastinating.'

'Do not justify your actions, Nithya! You have let me down ...'

'Giridhar is a hard worker, Ma. He has promised to return the jewels soon and I am sure he will keep his word. Actually ... it is for my sake that he is exerting himself so much ... he wishes to improve his social status which is why he is establishing his own pizza center. And Ma ... I like him so much and when I expressed my love to him a few weeks ago, he said he was also having the same feelings towards me. He further said that he would meet with you to formally ask for my hand.'

'Nithya, I don't want to hear another word. Tell him to come here immediately with the jewellery box. I want all my jewels back right now!'

Frightened by her outburst, Nithya said rather hesitantly, 'Ma, his cell phone is switched off –'

Parvathi's heart lurched. 'switched off? Since when?'

'Ma ... actually...on the day I gave him my jewels...'

Parvathi was in no mood to listen to her. She slumped on the sofa, clutching her head. 'Don't you see, you foolish girl, that bastard has befriended you for this very purpose. He conned you and has made off with our jewels ...'

Abruptly, she left the room and went straight to her husband's study. Raman looked up from his newspaper, startled.

'Just look at how your daughter has betrayed us,' Parvathi wailed. 'she has fallen in love with some pizza delivery boy and has given away all our jewels to him. Now that fellow has disappeared into the blue ...'

Raman stared at her, speechless. Finally, he said, 'Why would Nithya do such a thing?'

'It is all because of you. You have spoilt her silly. She has taken advantage of the freedom you have given her.'

'Whenever something goes wrong, it's always my fault! Aren't you responsible for your daughter? You never spend any time with her. You are always bringing home your work stress.'

Stung, Parvathi retorted, 'How can you say that! Everything I've ever done is for my daughter.'

Raman raked agitated fingers through his hair. 'We need to stop blaming each other and focus on how best to salvage this situation.'

'Talk to your daughter first. Ask her why she let us down like this. Then report this to the police and get back my jewels!' Parvathi shouted irately.

'Getting worked up serves nobody, Parvathi. Your daughter is not a child any more. We need to deal with this carefully. Give me some time to think this through.

Then, I'll talk to her. I'll speak to Kumar ; he has now become the Deputy Inspector of police. He'll be able to help us with this.'

CHAPTER SIXTEEN

Parvathi went to her room, still seething with anger. She lay down and closed her eyes, but sleep evaded her. Finally, she picked up a Tamil magazine lying on the bed-side table and flipped through it, mechanically. When she reached the matrimonial column, though, she sat up with interest. One advertisement in particular caught her eye.

'Thirty-year-old, manager in a multinational company, good salary, looking for an educated girl, no dowry expected.'

Early the next morning, she dialed the telephone number in the advertisement and waited anxiously. A lady answered her call and told Parvathi that she was in a hurry to finalize her son's marriage because she wanted to move in with her daughter and son-in-law, both of whom were employed, and help them out by babysitting her grandchildren. After an exchange of information about their families, they agreed to meet in person for further discussion.

The following day, Lakshmi came over to Parvathi's home. During their tête-à-tête, Parvathi summoned Nithya and asked her to bring beverages and snacks for her guest. She was happy to note that Lakshmi seemed to approve of Nithya. Lakshmi promised to return the next week-end with her son.

Parvathi was very excited about this alliance. The only reservation she had was the boy's age. He was ten years older than Nithya. However, she consoled herself with the thought that with age came maturity. He was sure to take care of her daughter with love and understanding. What more could a mother wish for?

That evening when Raman returned home, Parvathi told him of the new turn of events. 'see, god has not deserted us, after all! The boy's mother prefers a simple marriage and is not very particular about dowry.'

'And did you speak to your daughter about this?' Raman asked tersely.

'Not yet. I'll leave that to you. She listens to you. Tell her we are doing what's best for her. The boy is coming next weekend to see her. Convince her, somehow, to meet with him.'

'I'll do my best.'

CHAPTER SEVENTEEN

Raman was sitting in his room, twiddling his thumbs. He was not sure how he was going to tackle this unenviable task of breaking the news of her mother's decision to Nithya.

When her father summoned her to his room, she went with trepidation. Her mother had surely told him everything.

Raman gestured for her to sit down and said, 'Nithya, now that your studies are over, we should start planning for your marriage. A boy is coming with his family to see you next weekend.'

She stared at him dumbfounded. At last, she found her voice and said softly, 'Dad, I am not interested in marriage right now.'

'You're just confused now, my dear. Just listen to your parents. We only want what's best for you.'

'Dad, please don't force me into marriage now ... didn't mother tell you about Giridhar ...'

'You are too young to take such a decision for yourself, Nithya. We always do what is best for you, trust me.'

Gathering some courage, she said, 'Dad, I have indeed made the right decision ... I shall prove that to you. Giridhar is a good friend of mine and, in fact, he was the one who taught me to ride the Scooty and ...'

'Nithya, stop talking nonsense. Don't get carried away by this talk of love! It is all hogwash. By marrying the boy whom we have chosen for you, you will be much happier.'

'But, Dad, Giridhar is planning to come and meet you shortly regarding ...'

'Don't be so naïve, Nithya! Don't you realize he has made a fool out of you and has run away with our jewellery? He is never going to come back!' Raman was beginning to lose his patience now.

Nithya burst into tears. 'What if he does?' she sobbed. 'What if he comes back and I am already married? Wouldn't I be plagued by guilt for the rest of my life?'

Raman's heart melted on seeing his daughter cry. Getting to his feet, he said softly, 'How long do you wish to wait for him? Your whole life?'

'No, Dad, just give me a month's time.'

'And what if he doesn't return in one month?'

'Then I'll marry the man you choose for me,' she said, wiping away her tears.

CHAPTER EIGHTEEN

Mukesh was late for office and wondered why Nithya was not ready yet. He went into the kitchen and was surprised to see her still in her dressing gown over her nightie. 'Why aren't you ready for college yet?'

'I'm not going to college today,' she said, busying herself with clearing the table.

'And why, may I ask?' he frowned.

Nithya hesitated. All of last night, she had been vacillating between lying and telling him the truth. She had finally decided to tell him she was feeling unwell. However, on the spur of the moment, she changed her mind. One lie would inevitably lead to another and she would eventually end up in trouble. Without looking up at him, she said, 'I am going out to meet an old friend of mine.'

Annoyed, Mukesh said, 'Is your friend more important than attending college? You can meet her over the weekend.'

'Mukesh ... actually, it's not a she ... it's a he,' she said.

'A boy friend?' he asked.

Nithya decided she might as well tell him as much as she could. 'Please don't be upset by what I am about to say. Before our marriage, I was in love with him and we planned to get married. Unfortunately, he had to leave for his home town due to some emergency and my parents forced me into this marriage.'

Mukesh stared at her, stunned. At last, he said, 'Well, that's history now. Your love affair belongs to the past.'

Nithya said, 'Mukesh, his two sisters passed away in an accident. I want to convey my condolences personally. It wouldn't be right not to.'

Mukesh was not willing to let her go and he tried to stall, 'Nithya, please try to understand ... our desires are endless and we mustn't give in to them. If one desire gets fulfilled, another desire will immediately take its place. New desires will make way for newer desires as soon as they are satisfied.'

Upset, she said, 'Is it so wrong to visit someone who is mourning?'

'Nithya, stop arguing with me please. I don't want you to miss college and you are not going anywhere else. That's that. I am already late, so please get ready soon.'

His stubbornness got on her nerves and she shouted, 'You are so unreasonable ... I feel like a caged bird. I want my freedom. Give me my space. I am going out to meet him, whether you like it or not!'

Mukesh was furious now, but he controlled himself. She was a brat and nothing he said was going to change her mind. 'Nithya, please don't take your education for granted ... I am the one paying your college fees. Don't I have the right to tell you not to skip classes?'

Nithya shouted, 'I hate studying. I've decided to quit college ... you don't need to spend another dime on my education!'

'But you were the one who wanted to do your MBA.'

'That's because I wanted to take revenge on my parents. It was just a pretext to stay away from you ... to keep a distance from you. I never wanted this marriage.'

He took out his cell phone and said, 'Well, in that case, let me talk to your parents first. I am not sending you anywhere without informing them ...'

Nithya leaped forward and grabbed the phone from his hands, yelling, 'Don't drag my parents into this ... they won't let me go either ...'

'Nithya, give me back my phone ...'

Seeing the dangerous gleam in his eyes, Nithya thought it wise to return the phone to him, but added ungraciously, 'Don't you have any sympathy at all?'

'I should be asking you the very same question. First, you insult me by telling me that you were in love with someone and forced into marriage with me. And now, you are telling me that you want to go and see your ex-lover. Just who do you think I am? An emotionless block of wood? Now pay attention ... I don't really care whether you go to college or not ... but I insist that you stay put in the house!'

'I'm sorry, Mukesh. No one can stop me from going out to meet him.'

Grabbing her shoulders in a strong grip, he said, gritting his teeth, 'If you disobey me and step out of the house, you cannot ever come back again! Understand? I will not accept you back into my life! Have I made myself clear?'

Nithya said nothing. She stared at him defiantly.

When he left, she slammed the door shut behind him.

CHAPTER NINETEEN

What attracted Rajesh to Mahabalipuram in the first place was the fact that it was only fifty-five kilometres from Chennai and took him just over an hour to drive there. The town was famous for its temples and sculptures built by the Pallavas during the Chola period and attracted many tourists every year. Rajesh invested all his savings in setting up a hotel in Mahabalipuram and named it the Diamond Lodge. In time, he brought over his wife and son as well, and the whole family settled down here.

The ambience and the great quality of the food and service drew large crowds to Diamond Lodge and Rajesh happily thrived in this business, glad that he had taken the right decision in his life. However, now, after almost a decade, he could see that the temple town had grown decadent and degenerated. In the olden days, tourists flocked in to see the ancient artefacts and enjoy the expansive beaches and temples, but now, the temple town had become a den of vice and a hub for drug-dealers and prostitution.

Some of the guests who came to stay in his lodge requested Rajesh to arrange for a 'bed partner' which he had steadfastly refused. However, when his business faltered and the lodge's rooms remained unoccupied, he gave in. He hired a 'manager' to whom he entrusted the entire responsibility of handling the girls. The manager was good at his job. He trained the girls to receive the guests warmly and entertain them wholeheartedly.

Rajesh's decision to go with the tide turned him into an affluent businessman. Very soon, he developed good political links and managed to avoid police scrutiny.

Of late however, Rajesh was finding it difficult to meet the demands of his guests. For example, there was a guest in the lodge who was willing to pay a hefty sum for a very young girl, but there were none available. Where was Giridhar when he needed him? Rajesh dug out his cell phone and punched Giridhar's number.

CHAPTER TWENTY

Through the window, Nithya watched as Mukesh's tail lights disappeared around the corner of the street. She went to her room and changed into one of her prettiest churidhar suits. On a sheet of paper, she hurriedly scribbled the words 'I am leaving' and placed it on his desk before stepping out of the house. As promised, Giridhar was waiting for her at a bus stop by the house. The very sight of him set her pulses racing. It was as though no time had elapsed since their last meeting. Then, Nithya noticed that he now had an air of sadness about him which had not been there before.

Nevertheless, when he saw Nithya approaching, he welcomed her with a smile and handed her a box of pizza.

Nithya accepted the box, and looked up into his lean face searchingly. 'Giridhar, I am so sorry about your two sisters ...'

'Let's not talk about that right now. I am trying to take my mind off all that.'

'Come, let's have some coffee', Giridhar said and started walking to the Arya Bhavan Hotel nearby. They sat down in the corner of the spacious room, where they wouldn't be disturbed. After ordering coffee, Nithya opened the Pizza and offered a piece to him.

After a moment's silence, Nithya asked, 'Have you made any progress with your pizza outlet?'

'I've dropped the idea, Nithya. My mother wants me to settle down in Rajasthan. I came here just for you ... now that you are married, I want to return your jewellery and return home.'

Hearing this, Nithya felt vindicated in her faith. If only her parents had trusted her and waited awhile.

'Are you free for the day?' he asked.

She nodded. 'Yes, I have skipped college today.'

'In that case, can you come with me to Mahabalipuram?'

'Mahabalipuram!' she exclaimed, taken aback at the sudden request.

'Yes. The day after you gave me the jewels, I was on my way to the bank to produce them as security against a loan. That was when my mother called with the bad news. I was in urgent need of cash to go home and help my mother with the funeral arrangements. I immediately went to meet my friend, Rajesh, who runs a hotel in Mahabalipuram. I left the jewels with him for safekeeping and borrowed fifty thousand rupees from him before rushing home.' Giridhar took out a bundle of notes from his duffel bag. 'I have to return this money to him and retrieve your jewels.'

Noting her hesitation, he said, 'Nithya, if you don't wish to come, there's no problem. I can go alone. After collecting the jewels, I'll come to your house and return them to you.'

'My husband will return home by 6.30 p.m. I have to be home by then.'

'Oh, we should be back long before that.' Giridhar said, as he paid for the coffee.

'Cool. Let's go then,' Nithya said and climbed on to bike behind him.

It took an hour to reach the Diamond Lodge. When they got there, there was no sign of Rajesh. Giridhar asked for him at the reception. When he returned, he had a room key with him. 'Rajesh is not feeling very well, so he won't be coming in today,' he told her. 'I'll go to his house and collect the jewels from him. It won't take long.'

He then took out his cell phone and realized he had forgotten to charge it; it had run out of battery and turned itself off. Turning to Nithya he said, 'Could you lend me your phone, please? Mine's completely dead.'

'Yes, of course,' Nithya said, handing him her phone.

She rose to accompany him but he stalled her. 'You can freshen up and rest in one of the rooms. I won't be long.'

'I can wait here in the lobby, I don't mind.'

'It'll be more comfortable inside,' Giridhar insisted. 'Come, I'll show you to the room. Room number 20 is a special suite reserved for Rajesh's close friends and relatives ... and I happen to be one of them.'

Nithya followed him to the room, albeit reluctantly.

'You look tired after the long motorbike ride,' he said. 'You can perhaps even lie down for a while until my return or watch TV.'

'TV sounds good,' she said looking around for the remote.

Giridhar switched on the TV and handed her the remote. 'I'll be back in half an hour,' he said as he left, closing the door behind him.

As Nithya sat in the air-conditioned room, watching a thriller on the television, she completely lost track of time. Only when the credits began scrolling up on the screen, did she realize with alarm that nearly two hours had passed since Giridhar had left. Where was he? If they didn't leave soon, she would not reach home before Mukesh did. She rummaged in her bag for her cell phone before recollecting that Giridhar had not returned the phone that he had borrowed from her.

Nithya at once decided to call Reception and find out when he will be coming. The phone was dead.

She went to the door and turned the handle. It didn't open. She tried again. With a start, she realized the door had been locked from the outside and she didn't have the key.

CHAPTER TWENTY ONE

It was past midnight when Nithya heard someone at the door. She was lying on the bed, exhausted after banging on the door and screaming for help all day. When she heard the scrape of a key in the lock, she leapt to her feet. Two burly men enter the room. One of them locked the door behind him, while the other walked towards her. Tamping down fear, she demanded, 'Who the hell are you? Why have you shut the door? Where is Giridhar?'

Rajesh had earlier quarreled with his wife and left the house in anger. Once he reached the lodge, he opened his fridge and took out his favorite Johnny Walker. He didn't want to return home early so, he started gulping down one glass after another of the fiery liquid. When he was done, he sat back in his chair and immediately fell asleep. He slept undisturbed for five long hours and then suddenly woke up with a start. It was already past midnight. He fumed realizing that his wife had not bothered to call him up. Still in a foul mood, he decided to call his wife and yelled at her when he heard someone knock at the door.

'Come in', he said, his voice slurred.

'Just came to remind you that Giridhar's girl is waiting in the room.' Manoj said.

Though still quite drunk, Rajesh immediately agreed to take a look at her before leaving the hotel. Before handing over the girls to Manoj to be 'trained', Rajesh always made it a point to 'interview' the girls himself, so that they met the lodge's high standards.

But now, as he looked at the young, beautiful girl standing disheveled before him, her breasts heaving; his whiskey-soaked brain couldn't understand why she was behaving like this. Didn't she know why she was here?

Tilting her face up with a stubby finger, Rajesh said, 'Don't ask too many questions, baby. Your Giridhar is quite happy, I assure you. He's on his way home to get married to his pretty girlfriend and settle down there. Aren't you aware that he has sold you to me? I own you now. You have to obey and do whatever I ask you to do.'

The revelation cut through her like a knife. Giridhar! He had set up the whole thing! He had been deviously stringing her along all this time. What had she gotten herself into? She had to get out of here. Shrieking like a banshee, she ran to the door.

Rajesh, puzzled by her strange behavior, grabbed her and quickly dragged her back.

'You bastard ... don't touch me!' Nithya screamed trying to wrench herself free.

Slapping her hard across the face, Rajesh said, 'Don't act smart, you silly bitch!'

Crying, she squirmed out of his grip and ran to the door again and started banging on it hysterically.

Rajesh muttered something to the henchman who had stood by silently all this while. He moved swiftly, slammed the girl to the door, twisted her arms down and pinioned her hands back behind her back. He efficiently manacled her wrists together with metal handcuffs.

Although Nithya's stomach roiled, she wasn't ready to give up just yet. Mustering all the courage she had, she yelled, 'How dare you? Let me go out immediately or else ...'

Rajesh merely grinned, wondering all the while why this girl was enacting such a drama.

Provoked by this, Nithya screamed into his face, 'You bastard! Let me out of here now ... or the consequences will be really, really bad ... I'll make sure that you end up in jail ... let me go, now ...'

Chuckling aloud, Rajesh walked towards her and grabbed her breasts. Nithya backed off until she was right up against a wall. She was gripped with a paralyzing fear. Squeezing her breasts, he said thickly, 'What did you say, baby? I'm sorry, I didn't quite hear you.'

Helplessly, Nithya screeched in pain.

Rajesh repeated, 'Come on, sweetie, tell me what you said!'

Tears of pain and humiliation scalding her face, Nithya whimpered, 'Please stop ... I'll do whatever you ask me to do ... I promise.'

With a malevolent smile, Rajesh stepped back. 'Well, that's like a good girl.' He waved his hand, indicating his goon. 'This is Manoj, he is going to be your "trainer. He will teach you everything and tell you what you are expected to do. Cooperate with him and make things easier for yourself. If I hear any complaints, your punishment will be even worse, understand?'

Nithya nodded, trying not to let her knees buckle beneath her.

CHAPTER TWENTY TWO

Despite the desperation of her situation, Nithya's thoughts were very lucid and she realized that, in order to get out unscathed, she had to think fast and pretend to be meek. Therefore, when the 'trainer' closed the door and walked up to her, she knelt in supplication before him and pleaded with tears flowing from her eyes.

'Brother, please, let me go. I am not the type of person you think I am. I am a married lady and belong to an affluent family. It was my misfortune to have befriended that fellow, Giridhar. I lent him all my jewels to help him set up his own business. He disappeared for a while and showed up only now. It was only because he promised to return my jewels that I accompanied him all the way to this place, only to be duped again by that scoundrel. Now look at my plight.'

Hiccupping and sobbing, she continued, 'Brother, please, let me go. I will ask my parents to reward you. Please, please, have mercy on me!'

Manoj's feet were soaked with her tears. The helpless young girl's entreaties somehow touched his hardened heart.

This was a whole new experience for Manoj. The girls who were brought here by Giridhar were usually women who came of their own volition. This being one of Rajesh's conditions, for he felt that forcing girls into prostitution was a sin.

Manoj often felt sorry for the poverty-stricken women, driven by desperation into surrendering their daughters to him to 'initiate' them into the profession.

From Nithya's bearing and demeanour, it was obvious to Manoj that she belonged to a good family and he was baffled by his boss's savage behavior towards her. He had never seen him so wild. He was wondering why Giridhar had brought a clearly upper class young lady to this den of vice, when his cell phone rang. It was Rajesh.

Rajesh spoke rapidly, 'Giridhar has let us down. He has probably kidnapped this girl. We need to get her out of here quickly, otherwise we could get into unnecessary trouble.'

Manoj heaved a sigh of relief. Un-cuffing Nithya's hands, he said, 'Perhaps, god is with you today! Now listen carefully. My boss is ill and has just left for the hospital. In the meantime, I've decided to help you escape. Giridhar's thugs may be around and you may get into their mesh again. So, talk to your husband and ask him to come and get you as soon as possible. You have to leave unobtrusively without making a fuss. For heaven's sake don't inform the police, or I will get into serious trouble with my boss.'

'Thank you so much, brother. I will always remember your kindness, always,' Nithya said, quickly standing up and wiping her face.

As Manoj turned to leave, Nithya said, 'Brother, that Giridhar monster took my phone.'

Handing Nithya's cell phone back to her, Manoj said, 'This was given to me by the receptionist. Giridhar must have left it on her desk.'

Before dialing Mukesh's number, Nithya prayed, 'Dear god, please let Mukesh answer the phone immediately and not be cross with me and come quickly to rescue me from this hell-hole!'

CHAPTER TWENTY THREE

Mukesh was resolute. Nithya's heartbroken pleas to come to her rescue did not move him. He was determined not to help her for she had disobeyed him and had gone to rendezvous with her lover. There was no way he would forgive her or accept her back into his life.

Mukesh was about to step out of the house when his cell phone buzzed again. Irately, he picked it up to switch it off, then paused. It was his mother.

'Mukesh, I have been trying to contact you since last evening ... why was your cell phone switched off? Is something wrong?' Lakshmi asked anxiously.

Everything is wrong here. Ma! 'I had forgotten to charge my phone,' he lied.

'Why is Nithya's phone switched off as well?'

'I don't know,' he said, gruffly.

'Did you have a fight or something?'

'No!'

'Are you keeping her happy ...'

'Ma, I'm late for work ... if there is nothing important, can we talk later?'

From his exasperated tone, Lakshmi understood that something was desperately amiss. 'Mukesh my dear, even if she has done something wrong, please forgive her ... she is just a child.'

That really irked Mukesh, 'Ma, I said I've got to go. I'll call you back later.'

'Okay. Call me when you are free.'

Mukesh sat down on the sofa feeling bad for having been rude to his mother. He took a few deep breaths and tried to relax.

Thinking of his mother calmed him down. He quickly ran up to the bedroom and rummaged in the bin for the scrap of paper that he had crumpled and discarded in a fit of rage a few minutes ago.

CHAPTER TWENTY FOUR

As they neared their home, Nithya's heart raced. Mukesh had not spoken a word to her during the entire journey. He had shown up at the lodge and led her to the car, but it had been clear from his face that he did not want to hear about her ordeal or listen to her explanations.

Upon arriving home, Mukesh parked his car in the garage and walked into the house, taking long strides. Nithya meekly followed him to the door. Noticing that Nithya had not entered, Mukesh turned around.

'Can I come in?' she asked, in a small voice.

'Yes, of course!' he said dragging her into the drawing room.

'Why did you step out of the house?' he demanded slapping her hard across the face.

Her face stung so badly and she recoiled in fright. Tightening his hold on her wrist, he pulled her back. Following up with another slap, he asked her, 'Why did you disobey me ?'

'I am sorry for not listening to you, Mukesh, please forgive me,' Nithya said sobbing.

'Forgive you? What for? So that you can continue to ruin the rest of my life as well?' he sneered at her.

'Just forgive me one last time Mukesh...I promise to be very obedient and you will never regret your decision...,' she sobbed.

Unmoved by her request, he responded, "No way! I have had enough of you. We can never get along with each other.'

As Nithya stood there weeping, he commanded, 'Go and pack up your things and get out of here immediately!'

Whimpering, Nithya entered into her bedroom. She removed her clothes one by one from her wardrobe and dropped them into a suitcase.

When Mukesh was out of sight, she dabbed her eyes with her handkerchief and examined her swollen face. How many times her mother had warned her to keep away from that brute and how much she had hated her for that. Oh God! Infatuation is really such a terrible thing...a mere temptation...a fascination hard to resist. If only she had respected her mother's words, things would not have gotten this far.

CHAPTER TWENTY FIVE

It was 5 p.m. when Nithya finished her packing. There was no sign of Mukesh. She gingerly walked to the bedroom and heaved a sigh of relief when she saw him sprawled in bed, fast asleep. Hoping that he would be in a calmer frame of mind when he woke up, Nithya entered the kitchen.

It was the rattling noise in the kitchen that woke Mukesh. He got out of the bed immediately and went into the kitchen. Nithya was pouring hot milk into a cup.

'What are you doing?'

'I am making you a cup of coffee,' she mumbled.

Mukesh turned off the stove and said, 'There is no need for you to trouble yourself with me anymore. Go get your things and I will drop you off at your parents' house.'

Mukesh had not even noticed that she was wearing the new pink churidhar suit that he had bought for her birthday. She picked up her suitcase and examined her face in the hallway mirror. Although she was pink-eyed and her face was slightly blotchy from crying, she looked gorgeous in her new dress. It seemed hard to believe that, but for the grace of god, she could, at this very moment, have been sold into prostitution. It seemed a miracle that she had managed to return home. Home! Yes, this was her home, all the more precious now since she had thought she had lost it. Come what may, she would not lose it again.

On an impulse, she dropped her cases, ran up to the bedroom and climbed into bed, pulling the covers over her head.

Mukesh, who had been waiting impatiently for Nithya in the car, wondered what was keeping her. He noticed the luggage on the floor in the hallway and went to look for her in the bedroom.

She wasn't there and so Mukesh went from one room to another in search of her. When he could not find her anywhere, he knocked at the bathroom door several times only to find that the door was latched from outside. He stood there wondering where she might have gone when suddenly a realization struck him. It was not his habit to leave his bed unmade or in shambles. But there it was, the sheets and blanket in a bundle.

He yanked off the sheets and there was Nithya, curled into a foetal position.

She sat up and spoke in a rush to forestall any interruption, 'Mukesh, please, please, listen to me. Although I was not interested in this marriage, very soon I realized that you were a man with a heart of gold! Despite all my tantrums the problems I caused, you took care of me with great forbearance and patience. I fell in love with you so much so that, I began visiting the temple every evening after college. I kept praying that I should forget my past love affair and start leading a happy married life with you.'

Mukesh huffed, impatiently.

'No, please, hear me out. It was during this time that Giridhar, that evil bastard, called me and spun a yarn about a tragedy in his home and his intent to return the jewels to me. I stupidly believed his story. That rogue asked me to accompany him to Mahabalipuram because he had given the jewels for safekeeping to his friend, the man who runs the lodge. He conned me and took my phone before locking me in one of the lodge rooms. I've no idea where he disappeared after that. I think that room was sound-proofed because nobody seemed to hear my screams for help. Those people meant to sell me into prostitution. It is only by god's grace that I was able to escape unscathed from there ...'

Mukesh abruptly left the room and returned carrying the jewellery case in his hand. Putting it down on the bed, he said, 'Was it for this stupid thing that you risked your life?' Nithya was dumbstruck. She opened it with trembling hands and found all her jewels intact. This was the first stroke of good luck she had had in a very long time. Perhaps things were starting to look up, she thought.

'How did this end up with you?'

'It would have been in your hands but for your silly pig-headedness,' he said.

Bewildered, Nithya stared at him blankly.

'I did not know that you had declared war on your mother! She said that she had tried to contact you several times but you were so determined to cut her out of your life that you blacklisted her number on your phone. The poor lady came all the way to my office to give me the jewels. She said that they had been retrieved by the deputy inspector of police who is a close friend of your father. The fellow – your ex-lover Giridhar was caught red-handed trying to pawn one of your jewels. Although I refused to accept the jewellery at first, she convinced me that you adore them. I thought I could give you a pleasant surprise on your birthday and hid it in my vault. Well, I should have told you about this before ... it might have saved you from this nightmare.'

Tears filled her eyes at the thought of her mother with whom she had quarreled so bitterly. Nithya impatiently wiped away her tears and scrambled out of the bed and proceeded to pick up her luggage in the hallway.

'Okay, I am ready.'

'For what?'

'You said you'd drop me at my parents' place.'

'There is no need for that.'

'Have you forgiven me?' she asked, lifting her face shyly. 'Will you accept me back into your life?'

'Yes, my dear ... but do I still have to behave like a perfect gentleman?'

Nithya looked away, coyly. He opened his arms, and she ran into them.